# PORTSMOUTH
NEW HAMPSHIRE

## A PHOTOGRAPHIC PORTRAIT

PHOTOGRAPHY BY

PHILIP CASE COHEN

NARRATIVE BY

SARA DAY

TWIN LIGHTS PUBLISHERS | ROCKPORT, MASSACHUSETTS

Copyright © 2018 by
Twin Lights Publishers, Inc.

All rights reserved. No part of this book may be reproduced in any form without written permission of the copyright owners. All images in this book have been reproduced with the knowledge and prior consent of the artists concerned and no responsibility is accepted by producer, publisher, or printer for any infringement of copyright or otherwise, arising from the contents of this publication. Every effort has been made to ensure that credits accurately comply with information supplied.

First published in the
United States of America by:

Twin Lights Publishers, Inc.
Rockport, Massachusetts 01966
Telephone: (978) 546-7398
www.twinlightspub.com

ISBN: 978-1-934907-53-5

10 9 8 7 6 5 4 3 2 1

*(opposite)*
Portsmouth Waterfront

*(frontispiece)*
Sailing past Whaleback Light

*(jacket front)*
South End

*(jacket back)*
Shipyard Sunrise
Sanders Fish Market

Book design by:
SYP Design & Production, Inc.
www.sypdesign.com

Printed in China

Along New Hampshire's tiny, 18-mile coastline, at the mouth of the Piscataqua River, is a unique seaport city, replete with stunning coastal beauty, authentic New England charm, and well-steeped in American history.

Settled by Europeans in 1623, Portsmouth is one of America's oldest cities and, like many New England towns, its namesake hails from across the Atlantic. In particular, the port of Portsmouth, England, whose captain, John Mason, first founded the colony nearly 400 years ago.

From its earliest days, Portsmouth flourished from its fishing, farming, and timber industries. Once a major shipbuilding town, it quickly became one of the busiest ports on the Eastern seaboard. As the import-export trade thrived, wealthy residents built grand homes—exquisite examples of Colonial and Federal architecture. Many homes are on the National Register of Historic Buildings and are official National Historic Landmarks. Others are now historic museums, where early-American portrait paintings and hand-crafted, period furnishings provide curious visitors a glimpse of what life was like in Colonial America.

Located just 50 miles north of Boston, today, Portsmouth is a lively hub whose coastal beauty, outstanding restaurants, art galleries, theatre, and endless cultural treasures can be found all along its pedestrian-friendly downtown. Known as one of the country's most popular tourist destinations, it's fitting that the National Trust for Historic Preservation included Portsmouth on its list of America's Dozen Distinctive Destinations.

Yet, with all its downtown vibrance, Portsmouth is also immersed in unique natural wonder and charming small-town flavor. It is a place where still creeks and quiet inlets reflect crystal blue skies and gently swaying grasses, inspiring artists and poets alike. A place where the sound of crashing waves and the distant hum of commercial fishing boats, heading in with a fresh catch, evoke the character of Portsmouth's locals who share a strong sense of community. A place where the past is preserved in well-worn brick, and the future is paved with an industrious and energetic populous.

From hard-working tugboats, to the freshest seafood, to weathered fish shacks, and more, photographer Philip Case Cohen captures the essence of this alluring place in vivid detail. Season after season, at work and at play, Portsmouth, New Hampshire is a New England gem like no other.

**Downtown Portsmouth** (opposite)

Windows are illuminated from downtown Portsmouth's signature brick buildings as a blanket of clouds cover the sky and coat the rooftops with a fresh dusting of snow. It's not hard to imagine this scene during the 1800s, when large wooden merchant ships filled the harbor of what was once one of the busiest shipping ports along the East Coast.

**Sanders Fish Market** *(top)*

A decades-old Portsmouth landmark, Sanders Fish Market is the place to go for the freshest lobsters, clams, and fish. Family-owned for three generations, Sanders provides delicious seafood to local restaurants, large seafood chains, and retailers. You can order online or stroll in and enjoy your seafood with a side of neighborly conversation.

**South Street & Vine** *(bottom)*

South Street & Vine offers an excellent selection of hand-picked wines and savory cheeses from around the world. Their friendly approach takes the intimidation out of selecting the perfect wine for your next meal. In business since 2000, the shop hosts wine tastings every Sunday and also offers select meats, crackers, olive oils, jams, and more.

**Tranquil Waters** *(above and pages 8–9)*

Moored in tranquil waters, lobster boats in quaint surroundings reflect a relaxing mood. When not at rest, these rugged boats are hard at work in the chilly New England waters—some hauling in over 300 traps a day. Even though it has only an 18-mile coastline, New Hampshire off-loads millions of pounds of lobsters and seafood each year.

**Summer Reflections** *(above and opposite)*

A morning stroll along a Portsmouth waterfront neighborhood instills a sense of nostalgia. A small shack, clad in weathered shingles and simple A-frame structures contribute to the character and sense of history here. Summer brings mild breezes and plenty of vacationers who come to celebrate the 4th of July and seasonal warm-weather activities.

**Peirce Island Boat Launch** *(opposite)*

A dynamic perspective from the Peirce Island Boat Launch draws the eye to the opposite shore, where riverfront homes bask in the morning light. In 1923, the city purchased historic Peirce Island for just $11,000. The 27-acre island includes five scenic walking trails, an outdoor swimming pool, and a boat launch that city residents enjoy free of charge.

**View from Peirce Island** *(above)*

Located across from Portsmouth's South End, Peirce Island's walking trails provide stunning riverfront views from 5 connecting outlooks. The historic island was the site where clipper ships were built during the 1800s and also the site of Fort Washington, which played an important part in both the Revolutionary War and the War of 1812.

**Shapleigh Island** (top)

Lobster traps are stacked on the dock at the north end of Shapleigh Island. With wide views of the Piscataqua River, the tiny island is part of an 8-mile scenic route locals refer to as "the loop." It begins and ends in the South End, with historic sites, fishing villages, the Portsmouth Harbor Lighthouse, and hidden gems waiting to be discovered along the way.

**South End Sunrise** (bottom)

A New England sunrise baths the South End waterfront in warm tones, perhaps a kinder, late-Autumn gesture from Mother Nature, as she prepares for a harsher winter chill.

### Tugging Upriver

Known for its swift, dangerous currents, the deep Piscataqua River is the borderline that divides Maine and New Hampshire. It is the third-fastest tidal river in North America. Tugboats pilot huge cargo tankers upriver twice a day during "slack tides"—when the incoming and outgoing tides balance out, making for safer navigation.

**South End Moon**

Like a scene from Currier & Ives, a golden orb casts a glow over a sleepy South End neighborhood. Inspired by these beautiful vignettes, artists flock to Portsmouth, where their creativity can be seen in downtown galleries and studios. It's no wonder Portsmouth was listed as one of *American Style* magazine's top 25 art destinations.

**Summer Hues** (top)

Reminiscent of an early colonial village, much of Portsmouth's South End remains unchanged. Narrow streets and brightly colored clapboard homes are part of the timeless Yankee flavor here. Over 20,000 New Englanders call Portsmouth their home, with the population rising considerably during milder summer months.

**South End Yacht Club** (bottom)

The distinct yellow building on Pickering Street was formerly The Chandler's Loft, where patrons would pick up a sandwich and marine supplies before heading out on the water. In a new chapter for this South End landmark, today it's home to the private South End Yacht Club, whose members and their guests enjoy prime access to back channel happenings.

**Sunset River Cruise** (top)

The *Thomas Laighton* motors toward the Piscataqua River Bridge awash in color during a sunset cruise. The ship's namesake was himself a colorful character—a poet, politician, and an entrepreneur who was keeper of the Isle of Shoals Light in 1839. Known as "lord of the Isles," legend says the large man is buried sitting up in a stone chair overlooking the sea.

**Scenic Industry** (bottom)

Portsmouth enjoys a vibrant economy with growing industry along its scenic waterfront and throughout the city. From biotechnology to software, healthcare, education, and more, a wide variety of businesses, large and small, add wealth and opportunity to an already bustling tourism trade.

**El Galeón Andalucía** *(above and pages 20–21)*

An impressive sight at the commercial fish pier on Peirce Island, the *El Galeón Andaluccía* is a replica of 16th-century European merchant and wartime vessels. The 170-foot-long, 495-ton Spanish tall ship sailed into Portsmouth Harbor for a week-long visit as history buffs climbed aboard and rolled back in time 500 years during this once-in-a-lifetime experience.

**Sea Fog** (above)

Whaleback Lighthouse is silhouetted in a sea of fog that takes on a fiery glow when illuminated by sunshine breaking through a thick cloud bank. Whaleback Lighthouse marks the mouth of the Piscataqua River, between New Castle, NH and Kittery, ME. Built in 1872, the 59-foot-tall lighthouse is still an active navigational aid.

**Whaleback Lighthouse** (opposite)

Monotones of rustic granite contrast a brilliant pink moon against a soft blue, early evening sky. In this stunning portrait of Whaleback Lighthouse surrounded by calm waters, artistry flows from the photographer's heart and through his lens as only Portsmouth's beauty can inspire.

**Gull's-eye View** (above)

An aerial view reveals Whaleback Lighthouse's seemingly precarious perch upon a rocky ledge. The first lighthouse was erected in 1829 and, although poorly built, lasted over 40 years. The recent structure, built with enormous, dovetailed granite blocks, was automated in 1963 and a radio-activated foghorn was installed in 2009.

**Moonrise** (left)

A full moon rises with authority over Whaleback Lighthouse and punctuates the ever-changing seascape. With its isolated location, Whaleback surprisingly had only a few long-time keepers. During the late 1940s, innkeeper Morgan Willis would, at times, overcome his loneliness by dialing zero just to hear the voice of the operator, whom he later married.

**Crashing Seas**

Breakers smash relentlessly against the sturdy granite structure of Whaleback Lighthouse. The rugged lighthouse has withstood brutal New England conditions for over a century. It is owned by the American Lighthouse Foundation and managed by the Friends of Portsmouth Harbor Lighthouses. Accessible only by boat, it is not open to the public.

**Isles of Shoals**

Comprised of nine rocky islands over 146 acres that straddle the Maine-New Hampshire boarder, the Isles of Shoals were named by acclaimed explorer Capt. John Smith in 1614. Grand hotels once graced the larger Appledore and Star islands during the late 1800s. Today, narrated tours of the islands are provided via the cruise ship, *Thomas Laighton*.

**White Island Lighthouse** *(above and right)*

The Isles of Shoals lighthouse is located on White Island, the southernmost of the island group. The covered walkway that joins the lighthouse and the dwelling has been destroyed several times by raging surf. White Island is now part of the New Hampshire State Park system. With support from a local student group, Lighthouse Kids, it is maintained by volunteers.

**Isles of Shoals** (top and bottom)

Salty air, warm sunshine, hollyhocks and lush greenery abound, highlighting the summer season on the Isles of Shoals. Located six miles offshore, the small, rocky islands were formed by a huge glacier that gradually formed a deep pocket of water. Historically, the islands were landing spots for indigenous fishermen as well as the first English settlers.

**Fair Winds** (opposite)

With a summer breeze filling the mainsail, sailors enjoy an exhilarating tour of the New Hampshire coastline. A favorite pastime for locals and vacationers, the Portsmouth area has a variety of sailing clubs along the Piscataqua River — from beginners to avid racers, and for those who appreciate maritime history through unique narrated sailing cruises.

**The Haley House** (top)

One of several structures that once stood on Smuttynose Island, the legendary Haley House was built between the late 1700s and early 1800s. Captain Sam Haley, Jr. lived in the two-room cape until his death in 1839. Poet Celia Thaxter, daughter of notable local Thomas Laighton, describes the Captain's days on the island, *"there with his spyglass, scanning the horizon and all within it, while the wind ruffled his gray hair and the sun shone pleasantly across his calm old face,"* in her book *Among the Isles of Shoals*. The quaint cottage spent years in disrepair until a traveling carpenter offered to restore it in the 1990s in exchange for a week-long visit for him and his family every summer.

**Gosport Harbor** (bottom)

Gosport Harbor provides safe anchorage for recreational boaters and local fishermen of the Isles of Shoals. The protected harbor is formed by the breakwaters that join Star, Cedar, Smuttynose, and Malaga islands. The surrounding islands are sparsely populated with the exception of a few summer cottages or homes of lobstermen.

**White Island Wildflowers**

Delicate wildflowers dance in gentle summer winds, while weathered clapboards are a reminder of harsher winds to come. The White Island Lighthouse was first erected in 1820. The wood-shingled structure was replaced in 1859 with the current 85-foot-tall, brick and stone tower. Managed by the Bureau of Historic Sites, it is the state's only offshore lighthouse.

**Thomas Laighton** *(top and bottom)*

Named for a colorful, 19th-century New Hampshire senator, the M/V *Thomas Laighton* offers narrated tours that detail the history of Portsmouth's seacoast regions, as well as party cruises and private special events. The 90-foot-long vessel is owned by the Isles of Shoals Steamship Company. She boasts three decks and holds up to 300 passengers.

### Oceanic Hotel

The original Oceanic Hotel was built on Star Island in 1873 by wealthy businessman John Poor. Destroyed by fire and rebuilt in 1876, the new hotel was considered very modern for its time, with plumbing, electric bells, and gas lighting. Visitors continue to enjoy sweeping views from the large front porch as they attend conferences and island retreats.

**Old Ferry Landing** *(opposite top and bottom)*

A popular eatery on Ceres Street since 1975, Old Ferry Landing serves up fresh seafood along with sweeping views of the Piscataqua River and close ups of Portsmouth's famous working tugboats. The existing building first served as a ferry terminal, shuffling passengers between New Hampshire and Maine before the bridges were built.

**Old Ferry Landing** *(above)*

Sweet New England lobster and succulent steamed mussels—a meal fit for a king is best enjoyed in the casual dining atmosphere at Old Ferry Landing. Served with a tasty cup of "chowdah" and their famous "Jimmy Juice" cocktail, there's no better way to enjoy delicious seafood than this.

**Portsmouth Harbor Lighthouse** (top)

This historic lighthouse was built in 1878 on the grounds of Fort Constitution, a Revolutionary War fort where Paul Revere once road to warn Colonists of the coming British enforcements. Also known as Fort Point Light and New Castle Light, the 48-foot-tall tower was built of cast iron—rare for its time.

**Portsmouth Harbor Lighthouse** (bottom)

Dwarfed in size, but not importance, a tugboat carefully navigates a huge cargo ship past the Portsmouth Harbor Lighthouse. Located on an active Coast Guard station, visitors can climb 44 steps and a 7-rung ladder to enjoy panoramic views every Sunday from May through mid-October.

**Painted Skies**

With a backdrop painted by Mother Nature's hand, a tugboat steams along the Piscataqua River, past Whaleback Lighthouse. The 12-mile-long river is formed by the confluence of the Salmon Falls and Cocheco River. The river's easternmost 8.8 miles form Portsmouth Harbor where tugboats, trawlers, lobster boats, and more share a safe dockage.

**Four Tree Island** *(top and bottom)*

A long, man-made causeway joins Peirce Island with Four Tree Island and continues around its perimeter, providing sweeping views of the Piscataqua River, the Portsmouth Naval Shipyard, and the comings and goings at the Portsmouth Fish Pier. The tiny island is part of acreage donated to the city by sisters Josie and Mary Prescott in 1940.

**My Mother the Wind** *(opposite top)*

A courageous mother and infant, carved elegantly in black granite, bare the brunt of harsh New England gales. *My Mother the Wind* was created by Maine artist Cabot Lyford. It was installed on Four Tree Island in 1975. The inscription beneath the massive sculpture fittingly reads "For those who sailed her to find a new life."

**Brewster's Bait and Tackle** *(opposite bottom)*

As reliable as the changing seasons, Brewster's Bait and Tackle shop has been a Portsmouth staple since 1900. Family owned for five generations, the quaint, weathered shack continues to be the go-to spot for anglers' provisions. It is part of the history, character, and charm that draws so many to this unique seaside community.

**History Afloat** *(above and left)*

From the 1600s through the 1900s, flat-bottomed barges, or *gundalows*, carted goods along the Portsmouth coast. The *Piscataqua* is a 70-foot-long replica of these workhorses of a by-gone era. She is owned and operated by the Gundalow Company, a non-profit bringing awareness to marine environment and maritime history though unique sailing tours.

### The Piscataqua

History buffs, sailing enthusiasts, and students of all things marine enjoy an extraordinary experience aboard a replica of a centuries-old gundalow, the *Piscataqua,* as she sails past the Portsmouth Naval Prison. The Gundalow Company brings history to life with daytime excursions, concert cruises, and sunset sails with informative guest speakers.

**Peirce Island** *(opposite top and bottom)*

Whether walking or biking along is trails, 27-acre Peirce Island offers picturesque views around every bend. In centuries past, the island was identified by those who lived there at the time. During the early to mid-1600s when Dr. Renald Fernald resided there, it was known as Doctor's Island. Ownership by the Peirce family was obtained in the late 1700s.

**Naval Prison** *(above)*

An impressive architectural specimen, Portsmouth Naval Prison on Seavey Island dominates the coastline. Built in 1908 on the grounds of Fort Sullivan, a former Revolutionary Fort, the concrete landmark otherwise known as "The Castle," imprisoned captives from the Spanish-American War and WWI. Closed in 1974, it is not open to the public.

**Prescott Park** *(above and left)*

Wealthy Portsmouth sisters, Josie and Mary Prescott, in an effort to beautify a dilapidated industrial area, purchased and cleared over 10 acres of waterfront acreage and donated the land to the city in 1940. Today, visitors enjoy strolling Prescott Park's brick walkways that meander under shade trees, past formal gardens, and bubbling fountains.

**Prescott Park** *(above and pages 46–47)*

Smoothed by decades of use, the brick pathways of Prescott Park are lined with clusters of black-eyed Susans and impatiens, and make for a peaceful respite from Portsmouth's busy downtown. A wide variety of plants and flowers are supplied by local growers and the greenhouses of the University of New Hampshire.

**Prescott Park** *(right)*

A spear fisherman in bronze poses victoriously at the center of this large waterfront fountain in Prescott Park. The fountain honors U.S. naval officer, Ensign Charles Emerson Hovey, a Portsmouth native who gave his life while serving in the Philippines in 1911. A bronze relief portrait of Ensign Hovey is displayed proudly at the front of the fountain.

**Portsmouth Naval Shipyard** (top)

The Portsmouth Naval Shipyard has been an integral part of America's military might for over 200 years, launching its first warship, the USS *Washington*, in 1814. From wind power, to steam engines to sophisticated, high-tech innovation, "The Yard" has mastered the progression of technology and is unrivaled in nuclear submarine repair and modernization.

**Portsmouth Naval Shipyard** (bottom)

Passing the Portsmouth Naval Shipyard, a tugboat masterfully guides a cargo ship weighing thousands of tons, controlling its speed and direction along the Piscataqua River. One of the country's oldest working seaports, Portsmouth waterways traffic over 5 million metric tons of cargo each year.

**Shipyard Sunrise**

Dawn breaks with dramatic hues, its reflection blending into calm waters like a watercolor painting. In the distance, viewed from the weathered wharf of the Commercial Fishing Pier is the Portsmouth Naval Shipyard. One of only four remaining naval shipyards in the U.S., the PNSY encompasses nearly 300 acres and has more than 5000 civilian employees.

**Commercial Fishing** *(top and bottom)*

New England fishermen have made their livelihood from the sea ever since Native Americans taught the first pilgrims how to fish. The freshest cod, haddock, flounder, lobster and more are provided by these hardy "farmers of the sea" to be served up in every waterfront restaurant in the city. It's hard to find a better place to dine than in Portsmouth.

**Harvesting Delicacies** (top)

Larger lobster boats, like the *Michele Jean,* fish 100 to 200 miles offshore where the crew will spend 7 to 10 days lobstering. They harvest year-round in sometimes extreme weather conditions and rough seas. Their delectable, fresh catch will be offloaded, processed, and delivered throughout New England and shipped all over the world.

**Lobster Tales** (bottom)

The *Kelly Marie*, a Portsmouth-based lobster boat, motors in with a fresh catch. Steamed, baked, or even fried, the *Homanus americanus* (American Lobster) is a sweet and very popular delicacy. However, in Colonial times, this mouth-watering crustacean was considered a poor man's meal and was used only as feed for farm animals.

**Lobstering** (top)

Lobster traps add a pop of color to a gray New England day. Lobsters are most active between June and December and more abundant in summer when they migrate closer to shore. Since it takes about five 1-pound lobsters to get just 1 pound of meat, hard-working lobstermen always make the most of the warm-weather season.

**A Day in Portsmouth** (bottom)

At a brisk pace, the lobster boat *Heather Leah* makes her way along the Piscataqua River past quaint riverfront homes and the "no-frills" eatery, Morrison's Lobsters. At Morrison's you can enjoy fresh steamed lobster "alfresco" on their cozy deck in casual comfort with a great view of Portsmouth's waterfront across the river.

**Farmers of the Sea** *(top)*

In Portsmouth, commercial fishing is not just a job, it's a way of life. New Hampshire fishermen haul in tens of thousands of pounds of cod, haddock, and other groundfish species each year. With the onset of catch-limit regulations, resourceful fishermen will sometimes switch to scallops or squid.

**Foggy Morning** *(bottom)*

Commercial fishing boats huddle together on a foggy morning at Portsmouth's Commercial Fish Pier. Even with access to some of the best fishing grounds in New England, fishing regulations, put in place in order to rebuild stock, have diminished the fleet putting a strain on an already difficult, yet fulfilling, way of life.

**Salt Piles** *(above and opposite)*

Mountains of road salt are stored on the waterfront to be distributed by the truckload to nearby cities and towns in preparation for winter's inevitable hazardous road conditions. Cargo ships deliver over 30,000 tons of salt per trip, traveling from South American salt flats for locally based Granite State Minerals, Inc. and the Morton Salt company of Chicago.

**Market Street Terminal** *(top and bottom)*

At the Division of Ports and Harbors' Market Street Terminal, massive cargo ships deliver everything from road salt and wood chips to machine parts, oversized power plant equipment, and other container cargo from all over the world. The busy terminal includes 50,000 sq. ft. of warehouse space and an 8-acre, paved wharf with rail access.

**Working Waterfront**

A massive ship looms against lavender skies, her stern boldly establishing she's a long way from home. Dubbed "The Gateway to the World," the Port of New Hampshire includes the deep-draft Piscataqua River, Portsmouth Harbor, and other navigable rivers. The day-to-day operations of this busy port make it an important part of the city's economy.

**Memorial Bridge** *(above and opposite)*

Dedicated to World War I sailors and soldiers of New Hampshire, Memorial Bridge is one of three that span the Piscataqua River in Portsmouth. Originally built in 1923, it was replaced by a new, state-of-the-art bridge in 2013, complete with sensors for traffic patterns and environmental conditions. It also conveniently allows for pedestrians and cyclists.

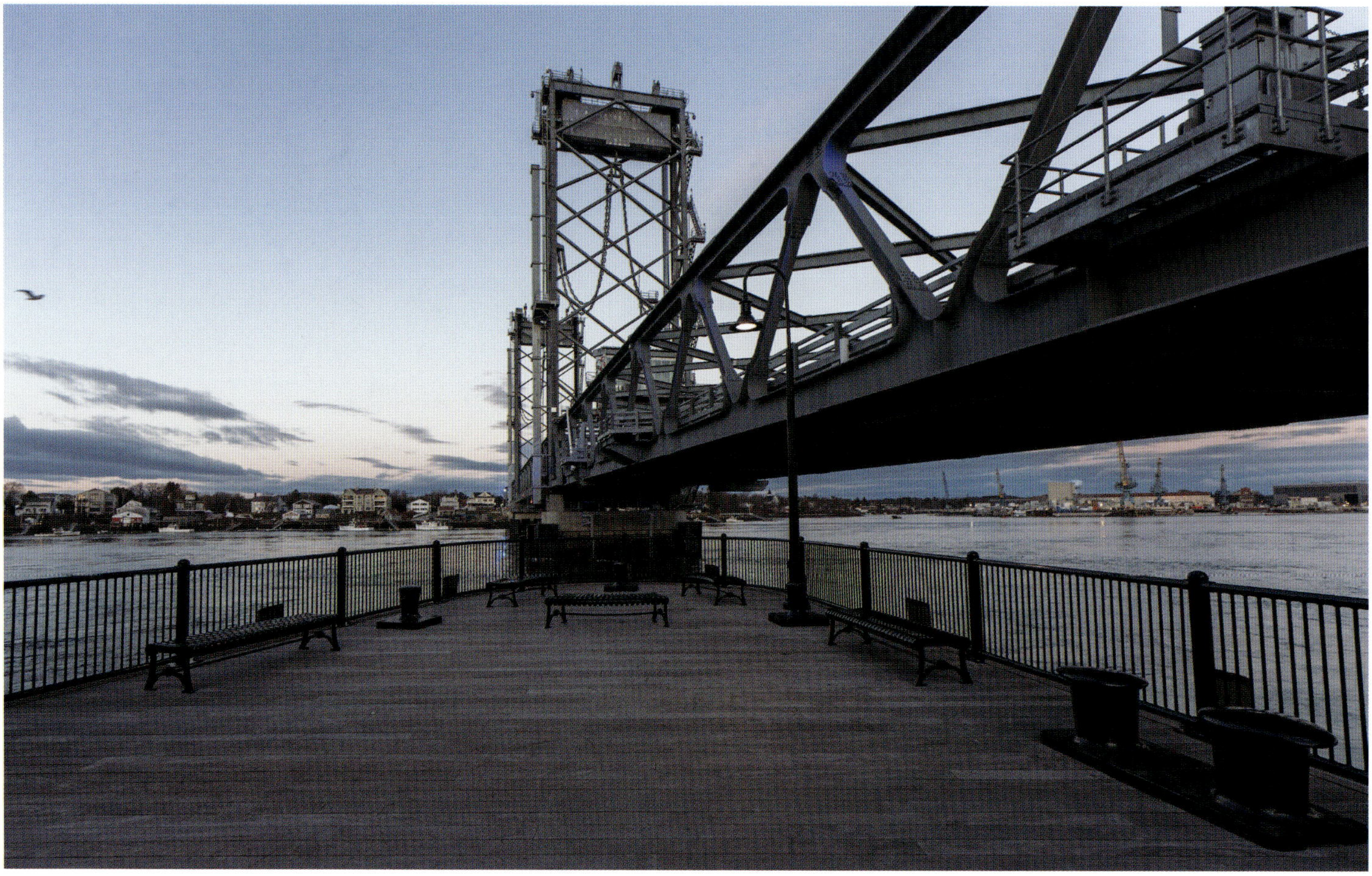

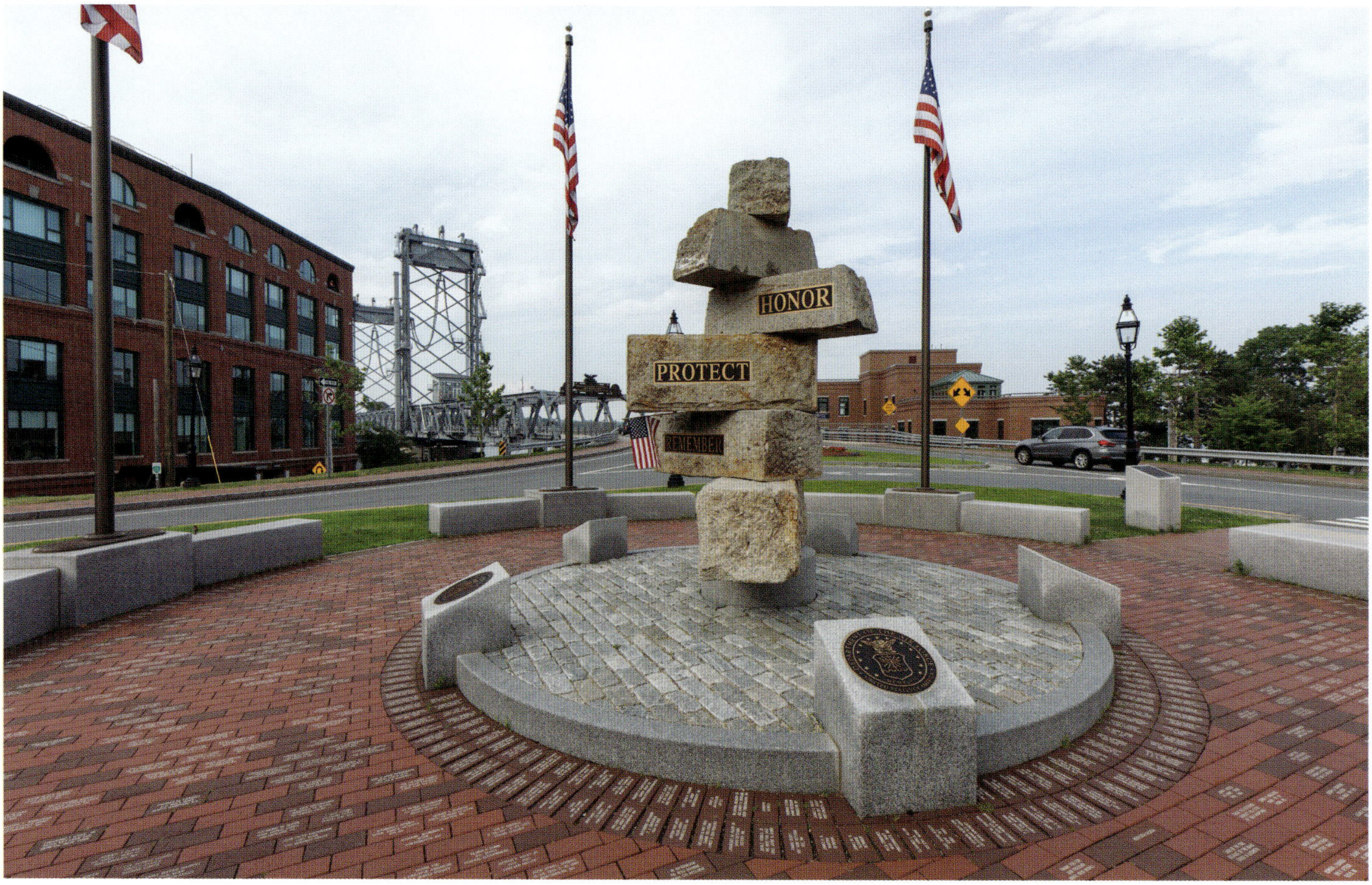
HONOR
PROTECT
REMEMBER

**Harborwalk Park and Pier** *(opposite top)*

Extending 72 feet over the Piscataqua River, Harborwalk Pier invites visitors to sit a while and enjoy a great view of Memorial Bridge and the comings and goings along the busy waterfront. Dedicated in July of 2016, the 2,400-square-foot pier is one of several 'pocket parks' throughout the city that help to make Portsmouth so pedestrian friendly.

**Veterans Memorial** *(opposite bottom and above)*

Three poignant words set in granite commemorate the rock-solid strength and courage of American veterans. The memorial's six granite blocks are from the foundation of the original bridge. Dedicated in 2013, the granite stack is surrounded by engraved plaques honoring each branch of service and each brick of the surrounding path bares the name of a local veteran.

**Portsmouth Book & Bar** *(above and left)*

Browse through hand-selected titles from poetry and fiction to children's classics as the aroma of freshly baked croissants wafts through the shop. Located in the historic old Custom House on Pleasant Street, Portsmouth Book & Bar offers a unique literary experience along with delicious small plates, beer, wine, coffee and herbal teas, and live entertainment.

### Custom House

Built in 1860, the old Custom House and Post Office was designed by Ammi Young, the same architect who designed the Custom House in Boston and the U.S. Treasury Building. The granite structure's stunning palazzo style is marked by its symmetry and decorative cornices. Today, the building is home to Portsmouth Book & Bar, shops, and offices.

**USS Albacore** (above)

Built in Portsmouth and launched in 1953, the USS *Albacore* now lies nestled in a place of honor at Albacore Park. An extraordinary design for its time, the compact underwater craft was used primarily for naval research and testing, and set the standard for future submarine design. The USS *Albacore* was designated a National Historic Landmark in 1989.

**Soldiers and Sailors Monument** (opposite)

Unveiled in 1888, the Soldiers and Sailors Monument in Goodwin Park honors Civil War veterans, with three sides dedicated to battles and the fourth, to the Portsmouth-built, Civil War battleship, USS *Kearsarge*. A portion of the pedestal that originally supported *Lady Liberty* 25 feet above the park eventually eroded and was removed in 1955.

**African Burying Ground** *(above and left)*

The African Burying Ground Memorial Park marks the site of a 300-year-old burying ground for Africans and their descendants. The site was exposed while roadwork was being done along Chestnut Street in 2003. The solemn monument, designed by sculptor Jerome Meadows of Georgia, honors the contributions of those long forgotten for hundreds of years.

**Sacred Ground**

Rededicated in 2015, part of the African Burying Ground Memorial features a group of bronze figures that represent a community who will continue to stand strong in remembrance of those buried on this sacred ground. Engraved upon each of the silhouettes is a line from a poem written by the memorial's sculptor, Jerome Meadows.

**South Cemetery** *(above and left)*

Located at the corner of South and Sagamore streets, South Cemetery is actually comprised of several burying grounds including Cotton's Burying Ground, Proprietor's Burying Ground, Harmony Grove, and Sagamore Cemetery. With its tranquil pond and meandering pathways, it's a peaceful place to stroll while observing historic markers from eras gone by.

### South Church

Built between 1824 and 1826 in the Classic Revival architectural style, South Church, with its familiar square belfry, was constructed with granite blocks from the quarries of Rockport, Massachusetts. Formed in 1713, today the church has a Unitarian Universalist congregation, diverse in beliefs and dedicated to serving the community.

**North Church 4th of July** *(above)*

With a backdrop highlighted by a burst of patriotism, North Church stands as a beacon on the Portsmouth skyline during an Independence Day celebration. The spire, dubbed "Portsmouth's landmark of record," can be seen from almost every city local, as well as from across the Piscataqua River in Maine.

**North Church** *(left and opposite)*

Built in 1855, its clock tower keeping time steadfastly for decades, historic North Church in Market Square had humble beginnings in a log cabin in 1641. Its many memorable worshippers include President George Washington, notable politician Daniel Webster, and Revolutionary War naval commander John Paul Jones.

**Odd Fellows Hall** *(above)*

Well-preserved, centuries-old brick buildings stand at attention along Congress Street. The building in the foreground was erected in 1878 by Frank Jones and was originally called the National Block. It was purchased and renamed in 1919 by the Independent Order of Odd Fellows.

**Old City Hall** *(right)*

Located at the corner of Daniel and Chapel streets, the Old City Hall building was constructed in 1858 and housed the Portsmouth High School for nearly 50 years, after which it became Portsmouth City Hall. Today, the building is used as office condominiums.

**Immaculate Conception Church** *(opposite)*

Immaculate Conception is one of three Roman Catholic churches in Portsmouth that comprise Corpus Christi Parish. Originally established in 1851 as St. Mary's, Immaculate Conception was Portsmouth's first parish. It is known as the "mother church" of St. Catherine of Sienna and St. James parishes.

**Portsmouth Athenæum**

Incorporated in 1817, the Portsmouth Athenæum is located at the heart of downtown in Market Square. Named for the goddess of wisdom, Athena, and her ancient Greek temple namesake, the Athenæum is a non-profit membership library dedicated to preserving local seaport history through its extensive collection, exhibits, and events.

**Inside the Athenæum** *(above and right)*

Details of this major historic seaport are well preserved inside the Portsmouth Athenæum. From sailing merchant ships to the movers and shakers of their time, maritime history enthusiasts will savor an authentic experience through an extensive collection of period art, historical artifacts, manuscripts, books, and photographs.

**Market Square**

Marked by its distinct red-brick buildings and bustling shops and restaurants, Market Square is the heart of downtown Portsmouth. The revitalization that took place during the 1970s is celebrated every second Saturday of June on Market Square Day, when more than 60,000 people gather to enjoy festive entertainment and activities.

**Early 19th-Century Architecture**

Part of the local Historic District, highlighted by the Portsmouth Athenæum, Market Square is a superb living example of early 19th-century New England architecture. Many of the distinct red-brick buildings in downtown Portsmouth were built in the early 1800s when a trio of fires destroyed many of the structures in 1802, 1806, and 1813.

**Horse and Carriage Ride** *(top)*

Warm summer months bring approximately two million visitors to Portsmouth to take full advantage of the city's unique offerings and historic charm. Whether sailing along its pristine coastline, taking in a maritime museum, or enjoying a leisurely horse and carriage ride through Market Square, Portsmouth is a fulfilling tourist treasure.

**Market Street Fountain** *(bottom)*

A bubbling fountain alongside shaded benches make for an inviting stopping place in Portsmouth's Market Square. The square, once a military training ground, features wide, brick-paved sidewalks that run along busy shops, galleries, and eateries. It was the first area in the city to be paved, done so in 1762 with funds from a public lottery.

**Rockingham** *(above and left)*

Built by Frank Jones in 1885, the Colonial Revival building on State Street was once the Rockingham Hotel. Its stunning architectural style was intended to resemble the home of Woodbury Langdon, whose mansion once occupied the same site. Now residences with entrances marked by Jones' signature lions, Rockingham is on the National Register of Historic Places.

**The Music Hall** *(above and right)*

Providing outstanding diverse entertainment for 140 years, The Music Hall on Chestnut Street received the *Yankee Magazine* Editor's Choice award for "Best Performing Arts Venue." With a 900-seat auditorium, it is New Hampshire's oldest theater and has acquired national recognition for restorations, after being saved from demolition in 1987.

**3S Artspace** (top)

Opened on Vaughan Street in 2015, 3S Artspace adds much to the flavor of this culturally charged community. Gallery exhibits feature significant contemporary artists in a modern, open space. Along with inspirational visual arts, 3S Artspace features outstanding music, films, dance, and events. The venue can also be reserved for weddings and private parties.

**Ale House Inn** (opposite top and bottom)

Formerly a warehouse for the 1876 Portsmouth Brewing Company, Ale House Inn is a unique hotel, with an ambiance steeped in local history, yet delivering all the modern amenities. Located on Bow Street, in the heart of downtown, guests are just a stroll away from Prescott Park as well as the fabulous restaurants and entertainment Portsmouth offers.

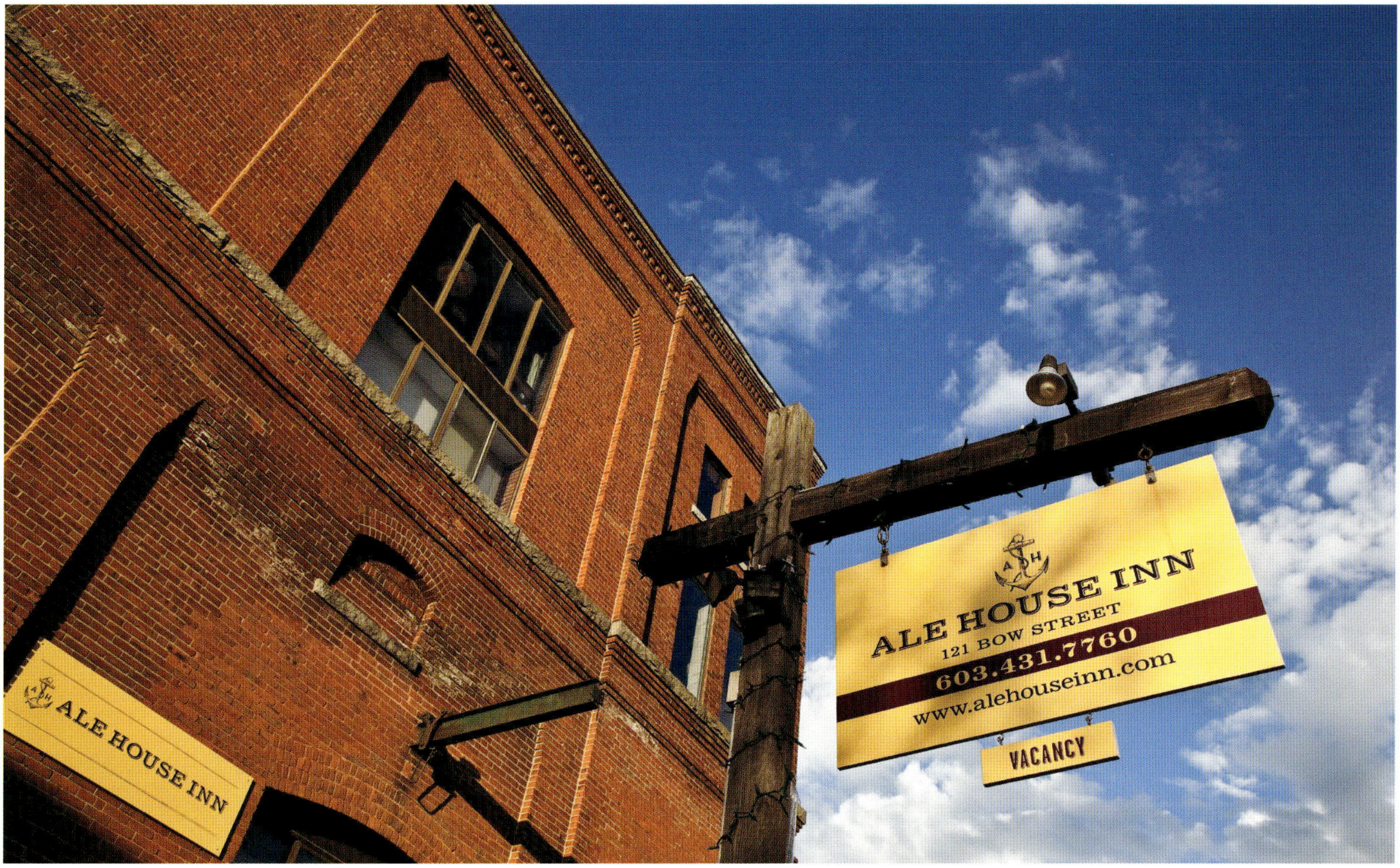
ALE HOUSE INN
121 BOW STREET
603.431.7760
www.alehouseinn.com
VACANCY
ALE HOUSE INN

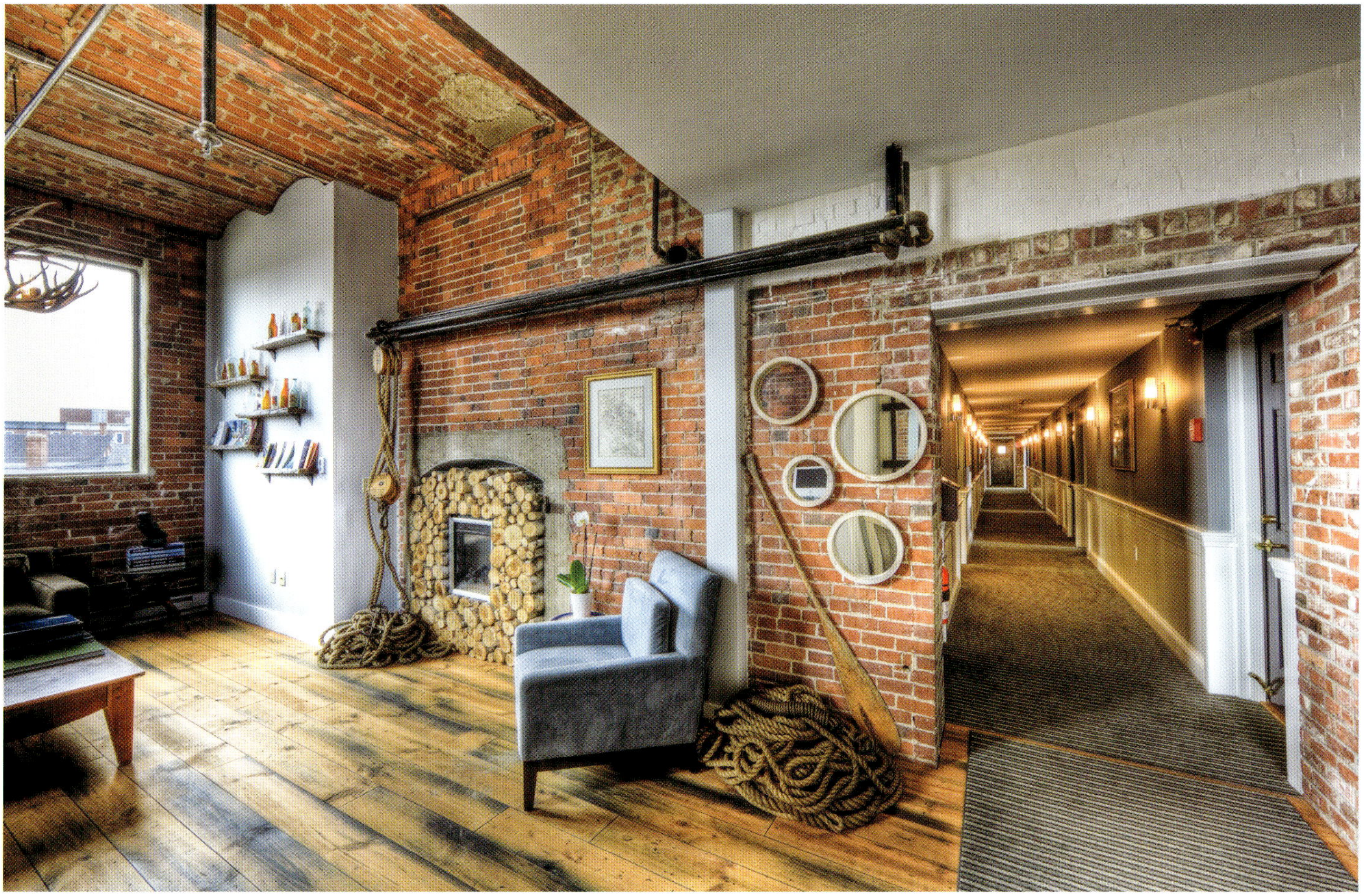

**Friendly Toast** (above)

Locals and others meet at the Friendly Toast where they can dig into creative menu items such as "Doughnut Stop Believin'" and "Kiss My Grits." The retro eatery on Congress Street serves up delicious breakfast, burgers, and healthy fare from local produce whenever possible.

**Portsmouth Brewery** (left)

A Market Street icon since 1991, the Portsmouth Brewery offers traditional hand-crafted ales, as well as some unconventional brews, alongside tasty fare. The Jimmy LaPanza basement lounge, complete with billiards and shuffle board, shares the same menu with the ambiance of a throwback, New York City lounge.

**Earth Eagle Brewings** (opposite)

Co-founded in 2012, Earth Eagle Brewings Brewery & Gastropub on High Street has a variety of beers on tap, including Wonder Guts, an adventurous brew made with locally foraged plants in place of hops. There are light appetizers to complement any libation; and music and events to round out the experience.

**Bow Street** *(above)*

The aptly named roadway that curves along the riverfront, Bow Street developed from what was once a rough, 18th-century path. The tightly aligned, worn brick buildings, built after the fire in 1806, are now home to artisan shops and eateries where patrons enjoy an unobstructed view of the comings and goings along the Piscataqua River.

**Commercial Alley** *(left and opposite)*

Intricately paved in rows and patterns, the lane that runs through a narrow canyon of red-brick buildings between Market and Penhallow streets is known as Commercial Alley. Pedestrian-friendly, the inviting tree-lined alley is home to an array of one-of-a-kind boutiques and restaurants that mark their address with stylish signage, beckoning passersby.

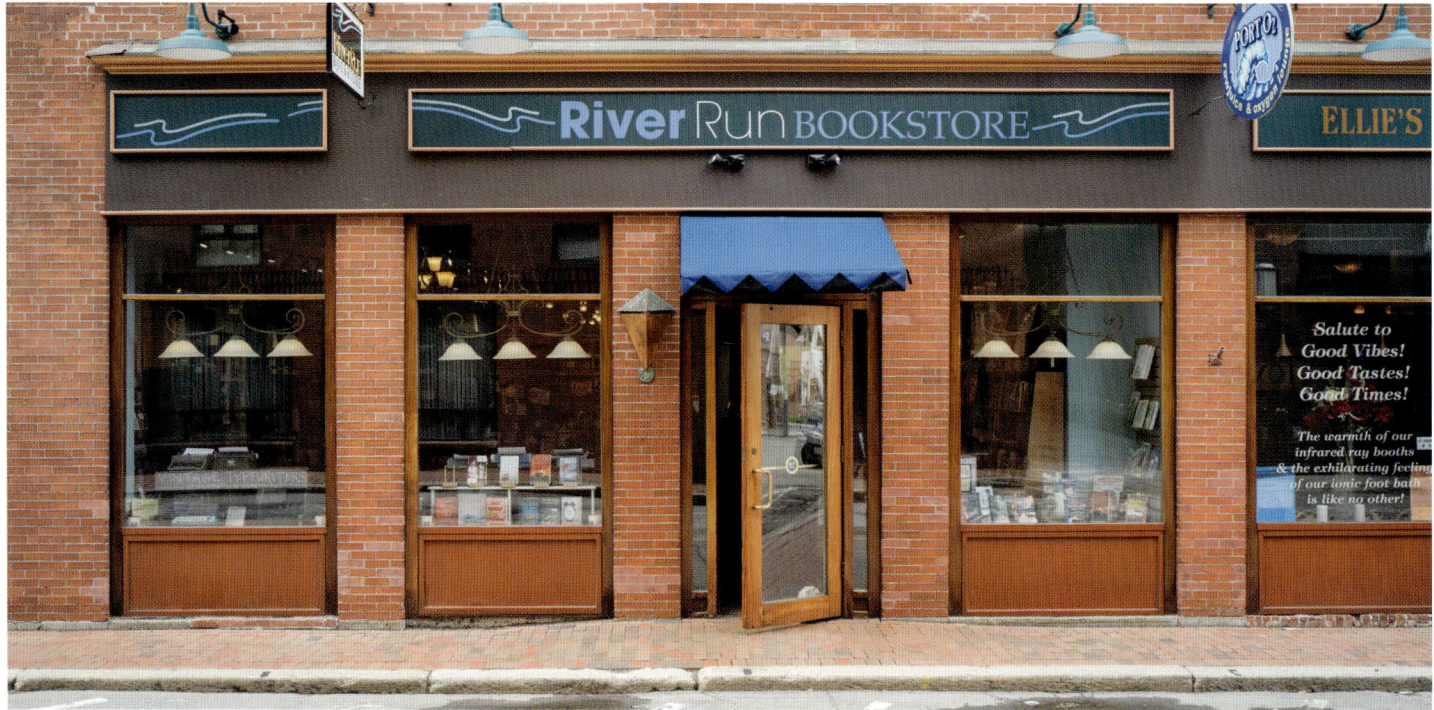

**Black Trumpet Bistro & Wine Bar** *(top)*

Along Portsmouth's waterfront, on Ceres Street, is the Black Trumpet Bistro & Wine Bar. The popular restaurant offers delectable fare with its fresh, seasonal menu. Patrons can enjoy a more intimate dining experience on its lower level, while the upper level invites friends for fine wine, lively conversation, and the same appetizing cuisine.

**RiverRun Bookstore** *(bottom)*

RiverRun Bookstore has a true passion for the written word. Along with choice titles, RiverRun offers inspirational workshops and thought-provoking speaking engagements with authors and illustrators. Additionally, RiverRun's Piscataqua Press project guides new authors through the independent publishing process that make their own books a reality.

**Downtown** *(above)*

Market Square is at the center of commerce in downtown Portsmouth, and the three streets originating from it—Market, Congress, and Pleasant streets—are brimming with offerings. Uncommon shops, galleries, and more provide a quintessential New England experience you'll find nowhere else.

**The Press Room** *(right)*

Portsmouth's source for live music since 1976, The Press Room on Daniel Street is well known for great food and live folk, jazz, and rock music, 7 days a week. Recently undergoing renovations, the iconic pub plans to continue its legacy of providing diverse, quality entertainment in a friendly atmosphere to a grateful community.

**Moran Towing**

Instantly recognizable by the large, white "M," a Moran tugboat pilots a huge tanker through the Piscataqua River's fast-moving current. Moran Towing Corporation was founded in New York in the 1800s. The company's Portsmouth fleet guides ships that, each year, bring millions of tons of cargo including coal, natural gas, and road salt to Portsmouth Harbor.

**Daybreak**

An unwavering channel marker stands at the ready for another day of busy traffic along the Piscataqua River. Red brick buildings along the waterfront cast a warm glow in the morning sun while the North Church spire pierces picturesque skies. It's daybreak in Portsmouth.

### Martingale Wharf (above)

A view of Martingale Wharf from across a calm Piscataqua River on Badger's Island. The Martingale Wharf building on Bow Street dates back to 1892, when it was used to house medicines and dry goods that were distributed along the coast. Today, it's the location of the Martingale Wharf restaurant, a casual, yet sophisticated bistro with world-class fare.

### Annabelle's on Merchants Row (right)

For more than 36 years, Annabelle's has been serving up tempting frosty delights such as Swiss Chocolate Avalanche and Mint Summer's Night Dream. Ice cream lovers can choose from dozens of delectable flavors, all made with the freshest, natural ingredients.

### Poco's Spiral Staircase (opposite)

Spiraling in a rhythmic, wave-like pattern, the fire escape behind Poco's Bow Street Cantina creates an interesting effect against dramatic sky and calm waters. Portsmouth's uniquely interesting vignettes, keenly captured by the photographer's creative eye, convey the authenticity and flavor of this extraordinary New England city.

**Vivid Sunset** (top and bottom)

Tugboats huddle in tight as dusk sets the sky ablaze in fiery tones along the Portsmouth waterfront. Evening brings endless possibilities—stroll along brick sidewalks to a favorite pub for handcrafted brews and live music; dine at one of dozens of exceptionally satisfying restaurants, or take in a glorious sunset cruise aboard the *Thomas Laighton*.

**At the Ready** (opposite)

The rustic charm of these hardy vessels adds much to the allure of Portsmouth's waterfront. Tourists delight in their photogenic appeal; notwithstanding, these familiar icons are always well prepared to pilot huge cargo ships along the challenging, fast-moving currents of the Piscataqua River.

**Martingale Wharf Moonrise**

The captivating beauty of this seaside city is reflected every hour of the day. Here, a full moon seems to rest momentarily upon a wispy cloud, as if to watch the glittering lights along Martingale Wharf pour streams of dazzling color into the Piscataqua River.

**Day's End** *(top and bottom)*

Day slowly slips into evening along an industrious waterfront. From commercial shipping to riverfront restaurants, Portsmouth's busy working seaport rivals that of Boston. Portsmouth's world-class industry and small-town feel make it one of the best cities to live and work in the U.S.

**Wentworth-Coolidge Mansion** *(top)*

Assembled from several preexisting structures, the 44-room waterfront farmhouse on Little Harbor Road was home to Benning Wentworth, the first royal governor of the New Hampshire province. It became an official New Hampshire government seat in 1753. Now owned by the state's Bureau of Historic Sites, it became a National Historic Landmark in 1968.

**An Artists' Retreat** *(bottom left and right)*

Between 1886 and 1954, the yellow clapboard landmark was owned by artist John Templeman Coolidge III who had significant Boston connections. Coolidge offered it as an artists' summer retreat. The footsteps of great American masters such as John Singer Sargent, Isabella Stewart Gardner, and Edmund Tarbell, will forever echo through its rooms.

**Wentworth-Coolidge Anchor** (above)

An enormous, 5-ton anchor is prominently displayed on the grounds of the Wentworth-Coolidge Mansion. Being both an artist and avid sailor, John Templeman Coolidge III had a keen interest in ships and was known to build models. Though its origin is unconfirmed, it is likely the anchor that came from the nearby Naval Shipyard.

**Lady Wentworth** (right)

No significant historic residence is without its scandals. Benning Wentworth's marriage to his second wife, Martha, raised more than a few eyebrows at that time—she being many years his junior and a house servant as well. The shocking proposal announcement was even documented in the poem *Lady Wentworth*, by Henry Wadsworth Longfellow.

**Wentworth-Coolidge Mansion**

*(opposite top and bottom)*

The 'choppy' architectural style of the Wentworth-Coolidge Mansion was achieved when several existing smaller structures were joined as one. The sprawling home was comprised of three wings—one for family, one for servants, and one for entertainment—each with its own separate entrance.

**The Hill** *(above)*

Once a close-knit Italian community, Portsmouth's North End neighborhood known as The Hill had been challenged with urban development during the 1960s and 1970s. Today, many of the historic, colorful clapboard structures have been repurposed as office space. Others were relocated to the Strawbery Banke Museum grounds.

**Strawbery Banke Museum**

History is well-preserved in the heart of Portsmouth at the Strawbery Banke Museum. Included on more than 10 acres are more than 30 historical buildings, most still on their original foundations. With over 30,000 artifacts and historical roleplayers in period costume, visitors learn what life was like in the Puddle Dock neighborhood from 1695 to 1954.

**Abbott Store** *(top)*

Take a trip back in time to Portsmouth's Puddle Dock neighborhood during the 1940s at Strawbery Banke's corner grocery store. The Marden Abbott House and Store is an authentic recreation of a friendly neighborhood grocery with no detail left undone, including Mrs. Abbott, the shop owner herself.

**Jefferson Street** *(bottom)*

The colorful wooden homes along dirt roads depict an era gone by at the Strawbery Banke outdoor living-history museum. Primarily of Georgian and Federal style architecture, the homes here were untouched by the fire of 1813, while areas north of this historic district were replaced with brick dwellings for which Portsmouth is now so well known.

### Strawbery Banke (above)

Walking the narrow lanes of Strawbery Banke, it's clear to see that, over the centuries, not much has changed. Named for the original 1630 settlement, this unique living-history museum includes many 18th-century buildings that are now used as museum houses or shops, while others are privately owned.

### Pitt Tavern (left)

Part of Strawbery Banke Museum, the William Pitt Tavern, located at the corner of Court and Atkinson streets, provided lodging and meals for weary, 18th-century travelers. The Grand Lodge of New Hampshire Masons, one of the oldest in the country, met here and for that reason hosted President George Washington during his visit in 1789.

**Wheelwright House** *(above and right)*

This classic, 18th-century, Georgian-style structure was home to Captain John Wheelwright, a seasoned seaman who commanded period cargo ships and privateers. As part of the Strawbery Banke Museum experience, the Wheelwright House is open to the public with cooking demonstrations held at the kitchen's large, open hearth.

**A Simpler Time** *(above)*

Roleplayers in period costume at the historic Strawbery Banke Museum depict a day in the life along Horse Lane in Portsmouth during the early to mid-20th century. Strolling this extraordinary living museum that spans centuries, visitors are likely to meet residents in homes, gardens, and taverns along the way.

**Cotton Tenant Houses** *(left)*

A successful grocer during the 1830s, Leonard Cotton built two rental properties in the Puddle Dock neighborhood. He owned over 40 rentals throughout Portsmouth. Strawbery Banke Museum holds demonstrations on weaving and basket making in one home, while the the other offers programs at its Horticulture Center.

**Lowd House** *(above)*

Built in 1810, this Federal-style home was the residence of Peter Lowd, a Portsmouth artisan and skilled cooper. Lowd prospered from creating casks, barrels, and kegs that were high in demand in Portsmouth's busy shipping seaport. Part of the Strawbery Banke Museum, the home exhibits tools of tradesmen who contributed so much to the region's growth.

**Historical Gardens** *(right)*

An ornamental fountain adds gentle splendor to the Goodwin Mansion Victorian Garden. Strawbery Banke Museum features several historic gardens including a Colonial Revival garden and hemlock grove, a Ukrainian vegetable garden, a 1943 Victory Garden, and several apple orchards. Strawbery Banke is listed on the National Register of Historic Places.

**Sherburne House**

Built between 1695 and 1703 by Captain John Sherburne, the Sherburne House is one of New Hampshire's oldest wood buildings. As an exhibit for Strawbery Banke Museum, Sherburne House introduces visitors to 17th-century building techniques and decorative details.

**Shapley-Drisco House** (top)

Built in 1795, Strawbery Banke Museum's Shapley-Drisco house is a duplex where on one side, Captain Shapley and his family live and operate a 1795 dry goods shop. On the other side of the duplex, the year is 1955, and the Pridham family are depicted living their American dream with a booming economy and a country at peace.

**Rider-Wood** (bottom)

Samuel Jackson, a Portsmouth tanner, built the Rider-Wood house circa 1780. Sold to John Rider in 1809, the home was both a family residence and small shop. After Rider's death, his wife Mary continued to sell molasses and other goods out of the shop and used her keen business skills to buy and sell land as well.

**Chase House** *(top left and right)*

Part of Strawbery Banke Museum's collection of historically significant buildings, the Chase House is an excellent example of Georgian-style architecture. Built circa 1762 by John Underwood of Kittery, it was purchased by Stephen Chase in 1799, a wealthy merchant whose family would reside here for generations.

**An Exemplary Citizen** *(bottom)*

Stephen Chase and his wife Mary lived quite comfortably at their Portsmouth home at the corner of Court and Washington streets during the early 1800s. An upstanding citizen, Chase was a Harvard College graduate, a member of the Portsmouth Federal Fire Society, and one of the founders of the original Portsmouth Library.

**18th-Century Sophistication**

*(top and bottom)*

Stephen Chase and his wife prospered from his maritime trade business and his efforts were reflected in the home's fine furnishings and décor. In 1883, the home was donated by Chase's grandson and was utilized as an orphanage for nearly 25 years. Today, the home is maintained by Strawbery Banke Museum.

**John Paul Jones House** *(above and left)*

Revolutionary War naval commander John Paul Jones was a resident at this Middle Street home in Portsmouth. Today, it is a museum filled with portraits, period furnishings, and artifacts that highlight his life and the Revolutionary War era. Maintained by the Portsmouth Historical Society, it is open from mid-May to mid-October.

**John Paul Jones House** *(above and right)*

Captain Gregory Purcell built this Georgian-style home in 1758. Commander John Paul Jones was a tenant in 1781 while he oversaw the building of both ships, the *Ranger* and the *America* respectively. Jones is well-known for his famous retort when asked during a battle in 1779 if he would surrender. His reply: *"I have not yet begun to fight!"*

**Wentworth-Gardner House**

*(above and left)*

Located on Mechanic Street in Portsmouth's South End, the Wentworth-Gardner house is an outstanding example of 18th-century Georgian-style architecture. The stunning riverfront mansion was built in 1760 by Mark Hunking Wentworth who gave it to his son Thomas and his bride, Anne Tasker, as a wedding gift.

**Wentworth-Gardner House** *(opposite)*

The fine details of the Wentworth-Gardner House were enhanced during renovations made by its new owner, Major William Gardner, in 1793. In 1940, a local committee purchased the home and the association, Wentworth Lear Historic Houses, was created to maintain the property. The home is open for tours, events, and wedding photography sessions.

116

**Governor John Langdon House**

*(above and opposite)*

The ornate carvings and attention to detail of this elegant, 1784 Georgian-style home on Pleasant Street was praised as Portsmouth's finest by President George Washington. John Langdon was a successful merchant, seaman, Revolutionary War general, and politician. A National Historic Landmark, the home and gardens are open for tours and on-going art exhibits.

**Oracle House** *(right)*

One of New England's oldest homes, the Oracle House was built in 1702. The distinct, peach-colored structure on Marcy Street was home to wealthy merchant and British Royal Navy officer, Richard Wibird. This home was also the location from which New Hampshire's first daily newspaper, *The Oracle of the Day*, was published during the late 18th century.

**Moffatt-Ladd House** *(top and bottom)*

The Moffatt-Ladd House, a magnificent riverfront, Georgian-style mansion was built in 1763 by wealthy merchant, John Moffatt for his only son Samuel. The Market Street home was also the residence of General William Whipple, signer of the Declaration of Independence. A National Historic Landmark, and a museum since 1912, it is open to the public from June 1 to mid-October.

**Moffatt-Ladd House & Garden**

The historic Moffatt-Ladd Garden was originally laid out by the Moffatts and significantly enhanced by A.H. Ladd in the late 19th century. After the house became a museum, the NSCDA-NH commissioned a Colonial Revival design. The formal gardens feature an 18th century English damask rose and a 1776 horse chestnut tree planted by General William Whipple.

**The Hotel Portsmouth** *(above and opposite)*

John E. Sise built this tasteful, Queen Anne Victorian home for his family in 1881. Successive family owners of the historic Court Street mansion added more rooms over time and, today, the home is now a 32-room hotel. With remodeling efforts carefully in keeping with the home's historic integrity, it opened as The Hotel Portsmouth in 2014.

**Warner House** (above)

This sturdy brick mansion on Daniel Street was one of only a few that withstood Portsmouth's 1800s fires, perhaps as a result of its 18-inch-thick walls. Built in 1716 by Captain Archibald Macpheadris, the home features four exquisite wall murals. These fine examples of colonial folk art are considered the oldest surviving wall murals in the U.S.

**Treadwell Jenness House** (opposite)

The widow of wealthy merchant Robert Treadwell had this home built on Pleasant Street in 1818. It was later occupied by state representative Richard Jenness in 1829 and then became a boarding house in the early 1900s. The brick mansion was once the site of the wooden structure, Brewster Tavern, a gathering place visited by President George Washington.

**Discover Portsmouth** *(above and opposite)*

Visitors are delightfully captivated by the thought-provoking exhibitions at the Discover Portsmouth museum and welcome center. From early-American masters to whimsical folk art, and more, the organization, operated by Portsmouth Historical Society, is an advocate for cultural art and is dedicated to the preservation of the city's rich local history.

**Discover Portsmouth** *(right)*

Discover Portsmouth is essential in navigating visitors and locals alike to the city's deeply rooted history, arts, cultural resources, and recent happenings. The nonprofit museum and welcome center on Middle Street has everything you need to know about historic walking trails, tours by land and sea, films, art exhibitions, and more.

126

**Richard Jackson House** (opposite top)

Richard Jackson, a Portsmouth farmer, seaman, and skilled woodworker, built the original section of this home on his 25-acre parcel on Northwest Street in 1664. With its post-Medieval architectural influence, at over 350 years old, it is the oldest surviving wooden home in the state of New Hampshire and a National Historic Landmark.

**Rundlet-May House** (opposite bottom)

Filled with fine furnishings and elegant décor, James Rundlet built this handsome home on Middle Street for his wife Jane and their seven children. The 1807 mansion was outfitted with the latest technologies of the time including a Rumford range, an indoor well, and coal-fired central heating. The home is listed on the National Register of Historic Places.

**Wentworth by the Sea** (above)

Originally built in 1874, the recognizable mansard-style turrets of this stunning hotel were created by brewery magnate Frank Jones. The grand hotel holds a place in American history as it is where the Treaty of Portsmouth was signed. Falling into disrepair and facing demolition in 1982, it was saved by the Friends of the Wentworth and reopened in 2003.

 **Philip Case Cohen** is a lifelong New Englander and has always had a deep appreciation for the region's history and its connection to the waterfront. Now residing in Portsmouth with his wife and daughters, he enjoys the pursuit of capturing timeless moments provided by the city's rich architectural and natural fabric as well as the greater New Hampshire seacoast throughout the year. Phil's primary goal is to transport people into the unique moments and places that he is able to capture through his work. To learn more about Philip's photography visit philipcasecohen.com.

 Award-winning graphic designer, **Sara Day**, never ceases to be inspired by the beauty and unique qualities of regions throughout the United States. A native of Gloucester, Massachusetts, Sara has enjoyed a long career working with publishers, photographers, and advertising agencies. She now resides in Vero Beach, Florida where she continues to use her talents to create exquisite photo journals and high-end promotional materials. To see more, visit sypdesign.com and www.twinlightspub.com.